Must Tell Jesus

Dr. Steven L. Bennett

Forward

I cannot remember not praying. I have had an ongoing conversation with the Lord since early childhood. I was surrounded by those who pray. My family, my friends, and my church prayed. Through the years, I have been refined in my praying by what I have learned. The people I have known, the Bible, the books I have read, and what the Holy Spirit has taught me is summed up in this book.

I wish that I could remember enough to give credit to those who wrote, spoke, and modeled prayer to me. My forgetter works much too well to hope for this. No doubt, this is familiar territory to many. I have prayed for the readers that the Holy Spirit will open up some new ground to enhance their prayer lives.

After over fifty years in active ministry, I have come to recognize two types of Christians; those whose prayers are answered and those whose prayers are not answered. Perhaps something in this volume will encourage one to pick up the burden of prayer again and learn the reasons God responds to our cry.

Since I began praying as a child, I do not think it necessary to learn all the theological ins and outs about prayer. One has to begin somewhere. No matter what your knowledge or experience is, my advice is to just pray.

Praying for Only One Answer – "Yes"
Chapter 1

I was attending a camp meeting as a teenager when I saw God answer prayer in a way that changed my whole perspective of prayer. There were about twenty-five hundred people in attendance at this meeting. The cost of attending the camp was two dollars for a week. That bought an insurance policy for those in attendance. The room and board was free based upon donations and faith. The food was served family style in a huge dining hall and the sleeping quarters consisted of bunk beds in dormitories. In the middle of this particular week, the camp director, Dr. Percy Ray, announced at the end of the night session that there was no breakfast food available for the next morning. He asked some to join him at the altar to ask God to provide for the morning breakfast. After he had prayed, he sent the large crowd to bed with confidence that there would be food when morning came.

When the morning arrived, we walked into the dining hall to the smell of bacon, eggs, sausage, biscuits, and other wonderful things. Everyone was amazed and wanted to know where food for over two thousand people came from during the night. In the first preaching session of the morning, the camp director told the story. In the middle of the night, someone knocked on his door asking to use the phone. His refrigeration truck had broken down right in front of the camp and he needed to call his boss. He was allowed to use the phone, of course. When he hung up the phone he asked Dr. Ray where he could dump the food on his truck before it spoiled. Dr. Ray asked him what type of food it was and he said it was breakfast food. He backed the large truck up to the camp kitchen and it was unloaded, cooked, and on the table the next morning with plenty to spare.

I had never heard anyone pray with kind of expectation and faith. My perspective of God's answering prayer was never the same after that morning. He had not doubted that there would be food on the table. He expected an answer speedily and got it on a miracle level. My eyes were opened to the possibility of praying in power and faith without doubting the answer.

An evangelist once wrote, "If prayer is asking, then the answer is receiving." Jesus said that if we ask, we will receive. I had been taught differently. My concept of prayer was that I was attempting to pry things out of God's hands by making a good case for why He should answer me. Crying, begging, or manipulation with self-pity was all acceptable elements in trying to receive a positive answer.

It was after years of praying with hope rather than faith that I came to realize from the Scripture that there was only one real answer to prayer and that was "yes". This answer to prayer is clearly taught in the Bible but sometimes difficult to achieve. Simply, the average praying believer has been taught that the answer to prayer is one of three: Yes, no, or wait awhile. These are faith killing traditions that do not hold up under scriptural scrutiny. With those possible answers, one wonders if there is really any use in praying at all.

Suppose you went into a restaurant for a meal. When the waitress received your order she said to you, "No, you don't need that". Or perhaps, "Wait until I think that you deserve it." Or maybe, "I'm going to bring you some hay instead." These will bring one to a point to where they no longer see any point in asking. What's the use? She is going to give you an answer you haven't asked for anyway.

The true answer to prayer is "yes". This answer comes from a heart searching investigation. For example, when the Apostle Paul asked for his thorn in the flesh to be removed, it was not. The thorn was allowed by God to keep him humble (2 Corinthians 12:7). Satan was allowed to torment him in this area of his life. Paul was asking God to reverse what God's will was. It was plain why the answer was not "Yes". The will of God would not support his asking. When we ask in God's will, the answer is always "Yes" (1 John 5:14-15). When we ask selfishly, the answer is not "yes".   When God does not answer my prayer in a positive way, I should begin a thorough investigation of why not? God should never be doubts. My motives, heart, and God's will should always be looked at. If I don't investigate and find answers to my questions, I may find myself angry, rebellious, complaining, prayerless, or with resignation to circumstances.

So, what qualifies a "yes" answer to prayer? So much of our praying is simply wishing and hoping. A positive answer to prayer stands on the promises of God. The promises of God are "yes" and "amen" in Christ Jesus (2 Corinthians 1:20) to the glory of God. There are so many admonitions to pray in expectation of receiving but all are based upon God's promises. We are told that whatever we ask, according to His will, we **WILL** receive (1 John 5:14-15). We have been assured that "whatever we ask, we receive from Him" 1 John 3:22. There is no, "maybe, perhaps, no, wait awhile, or take this instead." The true answer to prayer is "yes".

One of the prerequisites to a yes answer is a working knowledge of the Word of God. There seems to be a growing Biblical illiteracy in the generation of Christians coming up. The promises of God are found only in the Word of God. In order for me to pray in faith, based upon the promises that God has made, I must know what those promises are or else my praying will degenerate into hoping.

In order to get the proper answer to prayer, I must have the proper prayer when I pray. There are several factors that must be in place for a proper praying experience. The first being that prayers answered with a "yes" is the prayer that is prayed in the **will of God**. 1 John 5:14-15 has been mentioned already. It is emphatic that God answers according to His will. When I pray in His will, I have no controversy with God, no differing opinion about what needs to happen. I am in full surrender when asking in His will. This clears up the question between what He *can* do and what He *will* do. Few people doubt that He can, many are uncertain of whether He will. Knowing and praying in His will dispenses with that uncertainty.

It is a dangerous position to try to impose our own will in our praying. I was once preaching a series of services in Thibodaux, Louisiana. I accompanied the pastor to a local hospital for a ministry visit. An unchurched family that he had been trying to reach had a sick infant. The parents were very concerned for the baby's survival. When we arrived, a woman was in the room to pray for the baby. After she had laid her hands on the baby and prayed, she announced to the desperate parents that God was going to heal their baby that very day because she had asked Him to. I cringed at her declaration. Sadly, the child died before the next morning. The parents lost all interest in spiritual things. It is imperative to know the will of God in our praying.

A heart understanding and conforming to the values of His word brings me to a position of delighting in Him (Psalm 37:5). That delight creates within me a desire to know Him more deeply and to gain a heart understanding of His word. When I understand His word, I understand His will and ask according to what He desires. His desires become my desires.

Another promise of Jesus (words in red) reveals the place of God's word in our praying. *If you abide in me and my words abide in you, you will ask what you desire and it* **shall be done** *for you. John 15:7.* The value of praying within the confines of scripture is supreme for "yes" answers.

Since the Holy Spirit is the author of the Bible, we have His help in praying in the will of God. Romans 8:26-27 reassures the believer that the Holy Spirit knows how we should pray when we don't because He knows the will of God. All prayer must be **Spirit led**.

This is the reason that we are instructed to pray in **Jesus' name**. If Jesus puts His name on our prayer, it is as though we are saying that Jesus wants what we are asking also. Jesus and I are one in this request.

My prayer should be an **honest prayer**. I should be praying in the same measure as my need. If I need a hundred dollars, I shouldn't be asking for ninety dollars hoping to make up the rest somehow. Jesus said to ask for today's measure of bread that we need (Matthew 6:11). No more, no less. If I am praying for healing from cancer, than I am not going to ask Him to clear up my sinuses in hopes that He includes my cancer in the process. Pray precisely (next chapter) so that we receive precisely.

Faith is the foundation upon which God works in our life. Faith is the primary pleasure that God takes in me (Hebrews 11:6). Jesus said His work will happen according to our faith (Matthew 9:29). The Bible states that we will receive because of faith (Matthew 21:22). We know that faith begins with and is based upon God's word (Romans 10:17) which releases the revelation of His will to us. I believe because God said it. I agree with Him in my prayer.

I once had a friend who was dying with cancer. He loved God and had taught His word for years. When the doctor gave him his death sentence and sent him home to live out the rest of his days in a hospital bed, he asked me to pray for him. I told him that I would come one night and pray for him. One night about ten o'clock I arrived at his house. Danny, one of our men, was sitting with him. I leaned over his hospital bed and hugged him. I told him that I wanted to pray before I prayed. In a little while I would pray over him. I went into another room in his home with my Bible. I laid on the floor praying and searching the Word of God for three hours looking for a promise to base faith upon. I found nothing. At one o'clock in the morning I went back to him. His tired eyes asked me what conclusion I had come to. I told him that God had given me no indication that his cancer would be healed. His eyes filled with tears and he said that he got the same feeling when he prayed. I could not pray in faith without a word from God. I buried him only a few weeks later.

My praying must also be **properly motivated**. I have had some real squirrely prayer requests. James 4:3 reminds us that we ask without receiving because we ask amiss, so that we can spend it on our own pleasures. Here are some examples of situations that some people have asked me to pray with them about.

One lady asked me to pray that God would go ahead and kill her sick husband because it was too hard on her to take care of him. A man asked me to pray that God would prosper his business because he wanted to buy nice things. One lady asked me to pray that she would have a baby in order to try to salvage her failing marriage. Another asked me to pray for her husband to be saved so that life at home would be easier for her. These are selfish prayers and none of them were answered. Neither did I agree to pray with them for answers.

Finally, my praying should come from a **heart that pleases God**. 1 John 3:22 states that we will receive when we ask because we keep His commandments and do those things that are pleasing in His sight. How do I clear my heart to please Him? First, I keep His commandments by being faithful to what He expects of me. I must also clear up any sin that may be in my life. It is possible that I need to make a sin list because Psalm 66:18 declares that God will not hear me when I pray if there is remaining sin in my heart. To make a sin list, I should include anything in my life that is a contradiction of God. This list should take me back to unresolved matters in the past. Matthew 5:23-24 makes it plain that God wants us to make restitution for any matters that have not been made right. I have known people who have returned tools taken from a job years before that the Holy Spirit had reminded them about. Some have paid back debts that had never been paid. Others have made relationships right with family members or ex-spouses, parents, and business partners. Time doesn't make wrongs right, forgiveness does. In order to pray with a clear heart that pleases God, I must make a sin list, a restitution list, and repent for forgiveness in order for God to be pleased with my pure heart.

There is only one answer to prayer once we know the proper principles that prayer is based upon. That answer is "yes".

Praying Precisely
Chapter 2

Jo Ann was a friend with whom we attended church. Once, while visiting in her home, she mentioned that they were financially short that week and had a pressing bill that must be paid quickly. My wife noticed that she didn't seem very concerned and inquired about her pacific state of mind. She answered nonchalantly, "Oh, I asked God to provide for it so I expect it will come to the mail box today or tomorrow."

Many Christians pray for too many things at one time without being able to focus on the pressing matters. When Jesus taught His disciples to pray, He was very aware of their traditions of ritual prayer rather than heart felt, faith filled, specific prayer. He drew them out of their traditional praying and taught them to pray precisely.

The promises concerning faith filled praying are in place. Mark 11:24 (words in red) reminds us, "Whatever things you ask when you pray, *BELIEVE* that you receive them, and you *WILL* have them."

Definite needs call for definite praying. Suppose you entered a restaurant and said to the server, "Just bring me some food." Would you complain about what you received? I remember, as a child, riding in the car with my dad. The service stations in those days had full service. Sis Hawkins was the service lady at the station that he traded with. I can remember him saying to her, "Sis, give me four dollars' worth of ethyl. I never figured out exactly who Ethel was but Sis pumped his four dollars' worth. Suppose he simply said, "Sis, give me some gas." Would he be right to complain that she gave him too much or not enough? He was always very specific about his request. Do you ever go to the grocery store and say, "Give me some groceries"? We are usually specific enough to make a list of what our needs are.

When we fail to pray precisely, it reveals an insincere formality in our heart that God is not impressed with nor is He obligated to respond to. In time, this insincere praying may result in a sin condition that Jesus calls vain repetition.

Truthfully, life's needs come to in precise areas. Most of our needs arise in one of three areas: relationships, finances, or health. These are also the areas that Satan attacks most often in life. If our needs are specific, our praying should be specific to our needs. To disguise, minimize, or generalize when I pray accomplishes very little.

I have found indefinite praying to be a good spiritual thermometer. What if, every time I saw you, I greeted you with the exact same words as though I had practiced them over and over? Before long, you would come to realize that I had an insincere heart toward you. Indefinite praying reveals a lack of burden or faith in prayer. Empty hearted praying shows that I am ignorant of God's will, God's Word, and God's Spirit.

When I was a young pastor of a small church in Upstate New York, there was a fine man in our congregation who had lapsed into ritual praying without realizing it. Every time he prayed publically, he tended to close the prayer with this phrase, "And Lord, please forgive us of our many sins." It was exactly the same each time. I approached him after the umpteenth time of hearing this and asked him, "Dan, why do you have 'many sins' in your life?" He looked at me like I had slapped him. "What do you mean, Pastor?" I explained that each time he prayed, he was asking God to forgive his 'many sins'. He did not ever remember praying that. It was something he had learned from hearing others pray the same thing.

There is much teaching on praying in a precise way in the Bible. After reading the instructions of definite praying, we should never be satisfied with traditional prayer again.

The Scriptures teach definite praying for provisions. Jesus taught us to pray, not for some bread, but rather for a day's need of bread (Matthew 6:11). In Luke 11:5, as Jesus was teaching the model prayer, a friend goes to his neighbor's house to ask for, not some bread, but for three loaves of bread. He was very specific in his need. Remember, many call this the Lord's Prayer but it is not. The Lord's Prayer is found in John 17 when Jesus actually prayed in Gethsemane. The prayer of Matthew 6 and Luke 11 is the "model prayer". Jesus did not ask us to memorize and repeat this prayer but rather to pray in that manner.

The Bible also teaches us to pray specifically for the ability to accomplish God's purpose. The prophet Elijah prayed specifically through the drought, the rain, and the challenge to false prophets on Mount Carmel. Joshua asked specifically that the sun would become stationary (Joshua 10).

The Word of God also teaches precise praying for revelation of God's will. Judges 6 records Gideon's specific praying over the sign of the fleece. Daniel 9-10 tells of Daniel's fasting and prayer for twenty-one days for an answer. James 1:5 says we should ask for God's wisdom for our direction.

So, how does one learn to pray precisely? This process of change must begin by deleting indefinite objects from my praying. Jesus instructs, "When you pray, do not use vain repetitions as the heathen do. Matthew 6:7". It may feel strange but we should review our prayers to avoid being as the "heathens". What did you pray for last night in earnest? If we have trouble remembering, it was probably insincere. Which items in my prayer needs faith applied to it in order to see an answer from a pleased God?

If possible, I should also find God's will in my praying. It would be better to seek God's will about a matter for days and pray for minutes in that will than to pray for days about a matter without knowing God's will. Do you ever hear comments like these? "It's a good thing that we don't always get what we ask for." Or, "Be careful what you ask for." Or, "God may say no when you ask for that." These statements indicate that God's will is not being considered in prayer. Again

I direct your attention to 1 John 5:14-15.

I should mention here a truth that I learned years ago. That principle is that God only answers His own prayers. Prayer actually begins in heaven, not in my heart. There is a cycle that God establishes with me in prayer. This is how it works.

1) God allows a need in my life. 2) I call out to God in prayer. 3) God reminds me of or gives me a promise from His word to base faith on. 4) I cry out in prayer to God in light of His promise. 5) He answers my prayer in response to my faith in His promise. 6) I give Him praise and glory for His answer.

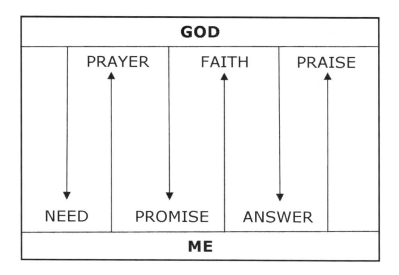

GOD		
PRAYER ↑	FAITH ↑	PRAISE ↑
↓ NEED	↓ PROMISE	↓ ANSWER
ME		

This is why Jesus said that the Father knows what we need even before we ask (Matthew 6:8). He has the supply before I have the need. He has the answer before I have the question. He knows the way before I become confused. He has the peace before I have the fear.

Finally, once I have purged my praying of insincere words and have found God's will in the matter, I will wait for God's answer. The only thing a promise from God needs to be fulfilled is time. God is not a fast food service. While sometimes He answers speedily, there are times when Satan hinders the answer (Daniel 10) or He proceeds to prepare us for the answer. Waiting on the Lord is a difficult thing for American believers who do not like to wait on anything. What I know is that you can trust the Father to always do the right thing. God answers prayers that begin in Him.

When our daughter and son-in-law were expecting their third child, we knew that it would be a little girl. My dad was a man of prayer. He kept saying that he was concerned for this child. He did not know why but he felt that there would be a problem to be dealt with when she was born. He was correct. When little Evangeline was born, she failed three hearing tests at the hospital before she went home at 48 hours old. Our daughter performed several simple tests to confirm her deafness. When the new baby was asleep in her carrier, the vacuum cleaner could be near her but wouldn't wake her up. Our daughter would clap her hands near her but there was no reaction. Her parents were resigned to accept God's will if He wanted her to be deaf. It was sad to them that she would not hear the voices of those she loved or hear wonderful music. But, they would be OK with whatever God desired. An appointment was made with a specialist to diagnose her problem. I suggested that we pray over her before the doctor sees her. I will not forget how her daddy cradled her little body in his arms, anointed her with oil and we put our hands on her and agreed together that we needed the Healer's touch. To the doctor they went and got a great report of no deafness. Somewhere between our praying in agreement and the testing of the specialist, the Healer answered and blessed. Today, music is one of her favorite things in life. Some would have an organic explanation perhaps, but it is my feeling that it is best to err on the side of giving God glory rather than to try to bring a natural reason to why something has changed. How grateful we are that God answers prayer.

Big Prayers – Big God
Chapter 3

Many people prefer a safe God. They also will only pray safe prayers to their safe God. C.S. Lewis once said that God is not safe but He is good. It has been my experience that most churches want a pastor who will lead them to a safe God. The miraculous tends to make nominal Christians nervous. No doubt, extremist have influenced the average Christian to avoid the extraordinary displays of power but I refuse to let charlatans keep me from believing in a great God Who is capable of powerful works. The age of miracles is not bound to the Bible days. The unchanging God stills likes to reveal His glory through powerful answers to prayer.

I embraced a life changing verse many years ago from God's prophet. "*Call to me, and I will answer you, and show you great and mighty things, which you do not know. Jeremiah 33:3".* I have seen this fulfilled so many times through the years. I could never go back to a safe God. I need more than safe in my life.

God has invited us to pray according to the size of our need. If our need is great, my prayer should be great. God has made provision for whatever size need we may face. Psalm 81:10 encourages us to "open your mouth wide and I will fill it." A big need gets a big response. Jesus said that "all things are possible to him who believes (Mark 9:23)." Does your need fit under "all things"? If our need is big, why should our prayer, faith, and expectation not be big?

When one reads the words of God to the prophet Jeremiah, there is only one conclusion to be made. God is a big God who does big things. *"Ah, Lord God! You have made the heavens and the earth by Your great power and outstretched arm. There is nothing too hard for You. Jeremiah 32:17".* Couple that with more statements about His greatness. *"Behold, I am the LORD, the God of all flesh. Is there anything too hard for Me? Jeremiah 32:27."*

God encourages the believer about His ability. *"Now to him who is able to do far more abundantly than all that we ask or think… Ephesians 3:20".* It is not possible for me to think of anything beyond God's ability to deal with. He has made promises about His ability and power. *"If you had faith like a grain of mustard seed, you could say to this mulberry tree, 'Be uprooted and planted in the sea,' and it would obey you. Luke 17:6"* The secret of the seed is in its potential. There is great possibility to those who have a mustard seed and are not afraid to use it. There are situations that arise that require powerful faith, not timid praying.

The Bible is rich in illustrations and examples of God's provisions for large needs. There are miracles that have to do with personal provision. A wonderful story of God's provision is found in 2 Kings 4:1-7. God's provision is important to every believer simply because a change of circumstances can happen quickly and take one by surprise as happened to the widow in this story. Setbacks come unexpectedly. Even so, desperation can be one of God's great teaching tools. Life is a consuming event and provisions are imperative. When life becomes a demanding creditor, it is important to have a never ending supply. As the old song says, "Little is much when God is in it." According to the account of the widow's plight, God can take what we have and make it work. God is not bound by our lack and we are not refused His plenty. According to 2 Kings 4:3, God works in the same measure that we are able to believe.

We are also reminded of God's miracles of personal protection. We find a great illustration of this in Hezekiah's life as recorded in Isaiah 38. There is also the dramatic deliverance of Hezekiah and his people from the powerful Sennacherib and the defeat of his army. At Hezekiah's prayer, one hundred and eighty-five thousand enemy soldiers lay dead at the rising of the morning sun. When dawn arrived, the breath of the men and horses were graveyard still. Lord Byron wrote a stirring poem, "The Destruction of Sennacherib" that details the death angel's work in the night that left an army dead by the glance of the Lord.

God has reassured us of His personal power available for operating in our life. Who can forget Joshua's command for the sun to stand still as he battled the Amorites? (Joshua 10:13). Or Elijah's show down on Mount Carmel with the help of the "God who answers by fire?" (1

Kings 18). There is also the account of Elisha receiving a double portion of Elijah's anointing to do greater works of the Lord. (2 Kings 2). I don't know that I have ever had a need greater than these manifestations. These are big needs answered by a big God.

Many Christians are living way beneath their privilege in prayer by being timid in their asking. There are actually benefits in asking according to our needs. The answers to big prayers is glorifying to God. Answering prayers that provide far beyond what we could ever do for ourselves, gives God an opportunity to manifest His glory. Since God only answers according to His promises, we should not expect it if God has not promised it. If He has promised it, there is no limitation to His power working in us.

Big answers to big prayers prosper God's work. I remember reading William Carey's admonition; Expect great things from God – attempt great things for God. These were concepts that kept him going as a missionary to India. God has a big vision for the life of the redeemed one. The only way to maintain this vision is by answered prayer. This allows us to live a life that is only explained by His answers to our prayers. It causes others to proclaim that He is, in fact, a great God.

The answers to big prayers gets believers what is needed to live life the way God has designed for it to be lived. We must pray according to our need. Even if that need is so huge that we despair except God come through with an astounding answers that we could never take credit for. There is so much more available to us than we ever tap into.

Sam was a former slave of a kind plantation owner. Even after his emancipation, he continued to work for the plantation owner. When the farmer died, he left Sam five thousand dollars in an account at his bank under Sam's name. After Sam had been on his own for several weeks, he needed a few supplies. It had been explained to Sam that he only needed to go to the bank and draw out what he needed as he needed it. On a day, Sam went to the bank to make a draw. His boots were worn down at the heel with holes forming in the soles. His clothes were mere rags. He asked the banker if it was true that he could get money for supplies at this bank. The banker said it was so. Sam wanted to withdraw fifty cents for a bag of corn meal. The banker was astonished at the small request. He told Sam that he was a well to do man now and could have new boots, plenty of food, and near anything he wanted. Sam only wanted a bag of meal. He wasn't used to being able to have what he needed in such supply. His restricted past had set his estimation of what the future must be. He left the bank with great needs, ignoring the great supply, and lived far beneath his privilege.

Our God has all that we need to live life the way he designed for it to be lived. There should be no timidity when it comes to prayer. God has all that we need and so much more. If our need is big, our God is bigger. Our great God desires to and is able to answer great prayers.

Praying In God's Will
Chapter 4

Janet was a fiftyish woman and part of our church. She loved the Lord and was a faithful attender but had not been deeply discipled. When God began to take our church deeper into His word, she approached me one night with a question. She had begun to hear others testify of God's grace in answering prayers. Some of those answers came to very difficult situations. I learned her story that evening. It seems that she and her husband, Tim, had been separated and divorced for about ten years. Their children were teenagers and lived with her. Neither Tim nor Janet had married other people. Both were single. They did not correspond or see each other except for issues with the children.

I could sense that she was very conflicted in her mind about her situation. With eyes brimming with tears, she asked if I thought God could restore her marriage after being dissolved for so long. I looked deep into her eyes in an attempt to discern her motivation. Loneliness? Finances? Pride? I could not get a good reading on her heart at that moment.

I asked, "What do you think?"

She said, "Of course, I know that God can do anything but I don't know if He will restore my home."

I asked, "What do you think would provide you with enough faith and assurance to pray for God to restore your marriage?"

She responded, "If I knew what God wanted, I would be settled about it."

I gave her an assignment.

"Go and search your Bible and see if you can find out what God wants in this. When you feel you know, let's talk again." I said.

Weeks passed but she did not mention her marriage to me again. She tended to be quiet and timid so I considered the matter as being over. One Sunday morning, after services, Janet approached me confidently. I was not used to seeing her so bold in her countenance.

"I know what God wants for my home," she said while both smiling and crying. There were traces of expectation in her eyes.

"What have you found out?" I asked. I didn't want her to feel as though I was toying with her searching but I wanted the conclusions to be her own.

"I know that it is God's will that my marriage be restored," she said intently.

"Where did you get that idea?" I tested.

"From my Bible! That's where you told me to look and I did," she announced. "I found that God hates divorce (Malachi 2:16). I also found that Jesus said that Tim and I are one and nothing should separate us (Matthew 19:4-6)."

She continued on with several more statements from scripture.

"So, you said you know God can restore your home. Does this give any indication that He will?" I fished.

She said, "I know it is God's will that Tim and I preserve our marriage. I also found, in 1 John 5:14-15, that God answers prayer that are is based on His will."

Janet had found the confidence and faith that she needed to pray in expectation.

Two years later, Suzie and I were reassigned to a new area. I lost contact with Janet and many others in that sweet congregation as life moved on. About five years after leaving the church where Janet attended, the new pastor of her church asked me to come back and preach a week of services. The first service was a sweet time of acquaintance with so many that we loved. In a few minutes, Janet stepped up to me with a gleam in her eye. She introduced me to a smiling man around sixty years old. She said he was her husband. I looked from him to her and then back to him.

I asked, "Is this Tim?"

She said, "This is Tim. I will tell you our story sometime this week."

I knew the story before she recounted it. God had answered her prayer and restored her marriage.

Praying in God's will is imperative if we are going to pray in faith. Any other prayer is merely hoping. There is no way that any believer can pray confidently without knowing God's will about a matter.

In learning to pray in God's will, it is best to begin with our Lord Jesus as an example. Jesus said publically that He came to do the Father's will. He said that He only does those things that He hears the Father say.

There was never a greater demonstration of the confidence Jesus had in prayer than at the tomb of His friend, Lazarus. In John 11:41-42, He said, *"Father, I thank you that you have heard Me. You **always** hear Me."* Who wouldn't want to reach a level of praying to where God always hears us?

In teaching us to pray with the model prayer, He instructs us to pray, *"Your will be done on earth" Matthew 6:10.* There is no other basis for prayer than the will of God.

The greatest demonstration of praying in God's will is a mysterious prayer in the Garden of Gethsemane. This part of His prayer is found in Luke 22:41-42. Jesus is praying with such intensity that the capillaries in His skin are rupturing and He is sweating great drops of blood.

He prayed, *"Father, if you are willing, take this cup from Me, yet not My will but Yours be done."* That statement was a confusing mystery to me for many years. I had heard others say that Jesus' flesh was weak at that point and that He was asking for a reprieve from the cross as though, at the last minute, He had gotten cold feet.

I knew in my heart that He was not flinching against what was to come because the cross was the very reason of His coming to earth. This had been decided before the foundation of the world (Revelation 13:8). To make atonement for the sins of men and to reconcile them back to God was His passion. Now, He wants to rethink the plan? I couldn't receive that as truth.

As I began to study this for myself, I discovered that God **did** answer His prayer in the garden (*You always hear me when I pray – John 11:42*) and removed the cup from Him. The confusion comes from misunderstanding what the cup was. The cup was not the cross, the cup was death in the garden THAT VERY NIGHT.

Jesus was the fulfillment of the Passover Lamb. In order to fulfill that important picture of sacrifice, Jesus must die on the same day that

Passover lambs were dying. The lambs did not die on Passover, but rather on the day before Passover. They died on the preparation day. Jesus did not die on Passover but on the preparation day. They had to get Him off of the cross and in the tomb before Passover began (John 19:31). So, while Jesus was dying on the cross, thousands of lambs were also dying all over the Jewish world at the same time. If He was to die that night in the garden, the type that He was fulfilling would be spoiled after generations of Jews had reenacted the scene each year.

Recall that Jesus told His disciples in the garden that His soul was sorrowful, even to death (Matthew 26:38) and He needed the disciples to battle in prayer against the spirit of death in the garden that night. Remember that when the mob came to arrest him, they came with weapons designed to kill. The spirit of death, Satan (steal, kill, destroy), was very active that night to derail the plan that had been established and typified in scripture centuries ago.

The final assurance that Jesus didn't lose a game of chicken that night in the garden is the passage (Hebrews 5:7) that declares that God heard Him in the garden and answered Him. The will of God was that Jesus stay alive until the preparation of the Passover the next day.

When we learn to pray in the will of God, the promises of God become "yes and amen" (2 Corinthians 1:20). Every praying Christian needs to know how to turn truth into reality by faith and prayer (Mark 9:23). Knowing the will of God and praying it (1 John 5:14-15) frees the believer to be fearless in His praying simply because he knows that God wants this too.

How is the will of God known in a matter? There are two aspects to the will of God. There is, first, the revealed will of God as written in the Bible. Here are examples of God's stated will in some areas.

It is God's will that:

People be saved. 2 Peter 3:9
That Christians be Spirit-filled.
    Ephesians 5:18
That Christians be sexually pure.
    1 Thessalonians 4:3
That Christians submit to spiritual
    leadership. 1 Peter 2:13-15
That Christians be willing to suffer.
    1 Peter 4:19
That Christians pray without ceasing.
    1 Thessalonians 5:17
That Christians delight in the Lord.
    Psalm 37:4-5

The list could continue as more directions and commands are taken from the Bible.

The other aspect of God's will is the unwritten will of God. How does one know God's will about matters not in the Bible? Is it God's will that you buy another vehicle, become a member of a certain church, or take an offered job? How does one know? There are five elements to take into consideration in determining the will of God that is not spoken of directly in the Bible.

The very first consideration is **God's Word**, the Bible. God will never contradict what He has written in His word.

I went to lunch with a man who had a question. He and his wife wanted to build their dream home. If he did, he would not be able to give to the Lord's work financially. He wanted to know what I thought. What I thought was that his mother must have dropped him on his head when he was a child. This man was a Sunday school teacher and a deacon in a church. What I saw was ignorance on fire. God would never release this man from Biblical stewardship in order for him to build his dream house.

If what is being prayed cuts across God's word, save yourself some time and stop praying that way. The word of God is the measuring stick for God's will. Since faith comes from the word of God (Romans 10"17), it is impossible to faith anything outside of God's word.

The second consideration in determining the unwritten will of God is the **Holy Spirit**. Jesus said the Holy Spirit would teach us all things (John 14:26). The Holy Spirit works in tandem with God's word and the two agree on all matters. The Holy Spirit knows the mind of God (Romans 8:26) and will lead us into the will of God.

One of the ways He does this is by putting God's peace in my heart about circumstances. Philippians 4:7 states that peace protects my heart. *"The peace of God, that passes all understanding, will guard your hearts and minds in Christ Jesus."*

To guard means to post a sentry at my heart. When I am involved with God's will, His peace will be in my heart no matter what the circumstances are. This means that no matter how bizarre something might seem, if God has put His peace in my heart, He is in that with me. No matter how logical something may seem (when has faith ever been logical?) and how wonderful it may seem, if there is something that just doesn't feel right about it, if my heart's peace is disturbed, it is better to back away. It probably is not God's will.

A third consideration is **Jesus**, God' Son. Would Jesus do this? Could this fit into who He is? If someone was to ask what you thought the perfect and primary will for a Christian's life was, how would you respond? Romans 8:29 reveals that God's primary will for the believer, the purpose for which he is saved, is to be conformed to the image of Jesus. This is God's primary will for our lives. His will, in the life of the believer, will enhance this conformity. Until the end of the Christian's life, God will be molding him into the image of His Son. When he dies, the final transformation will take place and he will become like Jesus (1 John 3:2).

A fourth consideration of God's unwritten will has to do with **God's work**. How does this matter affect what God is doing in life, in His church, or in His world? When the work of God harmonizes with the heart of God, all things within this realm can be permissible.

The final consideration has to do with **others**. How does this affect my life, witness, and spiritual influence?

Dan was a hard working contractor. He worked honestly and wonderfully with those who needed him. He loved the Lord and was faithful to church. He sat with me one day battling a decision. I let him talk.

"There is one thing that I really enjoy after a long day of work," Dan said. "It's a cold bottle of beer. Just one."

I didn't say anything, I only listened. I could see a battle going on inside.

"I'm not sure that is what God wants for me," he said. "So, I'm asking you, should I give up my beer?"

I decided that I would let the Holy Spirit continue His work in Dan's heart. I didn't say anything yet.

"For some reason I don't feel right about it. I know that one beer will not harm me. I'm not sure of what to do" Dan said.

I spoke. "Why do you think you feel confused about this?"

"What I am concerned about is my witness. I work with lost people and I don't want to be a stumbling block to them. I think that is why I feel this way," Dan confessed.

I smiled at him. I loved this man.

"It seems to me that you have your answer," I said.

"I guess I do," he said smiling.

I must consider how this matter that I am praying over affects the lost people around me, Christians, or the Kingdom of God in general.

To be successful in praying, the will of God is the primary key in receiving answers to our prayers. There are two kinds of praying Christians; those whose prayers are answered and those whose prayers are not. I am determined to stand back and watch His glory in answered prayer.

Praying in Agreement
Chapter 5

For years I prayed as though I had to convince or manipulate God and pry things out of His hands. Then, I learned that prayer begins and ends with God.

While one earnest prayer warrior can accomplish much, entering into a partnership in prayer enhances the power of prayer exponentially.

When God stepped out of heaven and became a man in Jesus, He followed a pattern that continues to hold value. It was His agreement with what God was doing in His developing years that kept Him moving forward in the plan that He had agreed to before the creation of the earth.

When He first arrived in Bethlehem's manger and up through adolescence, He agreed with obedience to the leadership that He had put Himself under. Namely, His parents guided Him in the early years (Matthew 2:12-15). He followed His leaders and was agreeable to that. Mary and Joseph were His parents. He was secure in that. His parents understood God's working in His life and they were secure in that. Later, He would put Himself under the Father's authority and leadership exclusively.

His public ministry was always in agreement with what God said (John 12:49). He agreed, without question, with God's Word, God's plan, and God's leadership. While we know that Jesus is God, the Fatherhood aspect of the Godhead took the lead and the Son aspect of God submitted in agreement to Him. There is only one God who is able to express Himself in three ways, all at the same time if He desires. We do not worship three Gods. When Jesus submitted Himself to the Father's will, His agreement with what He heard God say was so strong that He was able to use it as a sword of defense (Matthew 4:4-11).

Jesus was also in agreement with God's will. Glances at John 5:17, 19 and Philippians 2:8 reveal this. Agreement was a huge part of who Jesus was while on earth.

Because of Jesus' agreement with the Father, every prayer that He prayed was answered (John 11:41-42).

How do we partner with God in order to see answered prayer? The same way that Jesus did.

We first must find the mind of God and agree with it. 1 John 5:14-15 teaches that God answers those prayers that are in His will. Proverbs 16:3 insures that if we commit our ways to the Lord that our thoughts will be established.

We are instructed in Jude 20 to pray in the Spirit. Romans 8:26 declares that the Holy Spirit is ready to help us to pray. Praying with the help of the Spirit is the most powerful praying because He knows the will of God because He is God. That moves the praying believer into a new territory of prayer. Prayer, on this level, very easily becomes a matter of spiritual warfare. A prayer warrior must be prepared to battle for the will of God in prayer through the power of the Spirit. When one who prays with authority and power becomes a threat to Satan's kingdom, the devil will attempt to set up circumstances of defeat in that life. Agreeing with the Holy Spirit's victory, will see prayers answered, and glory devastates the devil. The believer who understands that Satan is a defeated foe will not be intimidated by circumstances designed to discourage prayer. The believer is more than a conqueror who acts like it, sounds like it, lives like it, and prays like it.

A very powerful principle of serious praying is agreeing with other saints in prayer. Jesus guarantees that, "*If two of you agree on earth concerning anything that they ask, it will be done for them by My Father in heaven. Matthew 18:19.*" One of the reasons for this is that it provides accountability in prayer. I have been approached by some who have wanted me to agree with them about some really flaky intercession. Selfish praying should be caught at this point. Some who want answers for their own selfish benefit can be stopped at this point by mature believers who refuse to agree with their request.

The other side of the principle of saint's agreeing in prayer is that if the need is real and agreed to; it can become a very powerful point of prayer. Leviticus 26:8 reveals the exponential factor in agreement. *"Five of you will chase a hundred and a hundred of you will put ten thousand to flight."*

God is pleased with faith (Hebrews 11:6). The tongue can be a faith builder or a faith killer. The praying Christian should use his mouth to establish faith by speaking the truth of God. Mark 11:23-24 illustrates this perfectly. *"Whoever says to this mountain, 'Be removed and be cast into the sea', and does not doubt in his heart, but believes that those things he says will come to pass, he will have whatever he says. Therefore I say to you, whatever things you ask when you pray, believe that you receive them, and you will have them."* Why does this passage use the word "say" three times and the word "believe" only once? We go on record and announce with our mouth only those things that we really believe. The tongue is a powerful faith builder. Listening to the word of

God preached, sung, or quoted illustrates this. We should not hesitate to demand that Satan release to us what God has given to us. We say with our mouth what God has declared with His mouth in order to stand in faith.

Once agreement and faith is established, the prayer warrior can stand against every work of the enemy, the devil. In order to quench the fiery darts of the devil, we will take up the shield of faith to fight with (Ephesians 6:16). With our mouth, we establish in our heart the will of God by reaffirming His promises verbally. These promises are not matters that we wish would be so but rather those matters that God has declared to be so. If you want God to speak to you, read your Bible. If you want to hear Him speak to you verbally, read your Bible out loud. If God has not promised it, don't expect it. When you can't find the words to speak for yourself, feel free to use His words. Speak His truth against Satan's lies. Stand strong in the face of the resistance by agreeing with other faith filled believers who will stand with you in agreement with God's Word and will.

Praying With Expectation
Chapter 6

Socks was our neighbor's dog but her master had died and she was orphaned. We lived on thirty acres of rolling pastures, ponds, and woods. We had dogs of our own and Socks kept her distance from our house. I could tell she was lonely and hungry. Our house sat upon a hill overlooking two large ponds. Our porch was deep and broad. At first, she approached the porch but never came up on it. In time, as she felt welcomed, she came up on the porch but never close to us. We fed her and talked with her until she eventually allowed us to touch her. Before long she was on the porch looking through the screen door at us. She had become ours. We kept her as our own until she passed.

The scriptures invite us to a similar approach to God as we pray. Psalm 100:4 speaks of coming before Him through His gates and into His courts.

Imagine His gates as being His porch and His courts as His front door. We do not just rush into the presence of God but rather approach Him with reverence and respect.

Socks came to us from her need of a master, food, and love. We could provide all that she needed. Our life contains earthly needs and heavenly expectations. Prayer is the connection between the two. How we enter into prayer is important.

In order to approach God in prayer, the will to praise must be activated. When Jesus was teaching His disciples to pray with the model prayer of Matthew 6, He taught them to approach God with high praise, "Hallowed is your name" (v. 6).

The Bible specifically points to the activation of our will in praise. Psalm 116:17-18 says, "*I will offer to You the sacrifice of thanksgiving and will call upon the name of the LORD. I will pay my vows to the LORD now in the presence of all His people."* There are similar passages like Psalm 34:1, "I will bless the LORD at all times." Praise is a matter of the will. Praise is not an emotional response to God but rather a chosen response to God.

Praise renews our strength like a spiritual transfusion. It drives away worry, frustration, tension, and depression. My grandfather once told me that if people would praise more, they would be able to clean out a lot of their medicine cabinets.

Praise empowers our prayer life (Psalm 50:14-15). Satan makes difficulties seem like impossibilities. He magnifies the negative. He makes us feel unimportant to God to the point that we feel that we cannot pray. Martin Luther once said that when he could not pray, he sang. Adoring praise warms the heart of God and gathers the worshiper into His presence.

Praise multiplies faith. When the need draws our focus and attention, something must bring our attention back to the adequacy of God. Praise allows our soul to soar to heights of faith that we normally could not reach otherwise. Praise not only helps our faith, praise becomes the evidence of our faith.

I do not pray because I feel like it, I pray because I ought to. When our son and daughter were growing up and approached the time to learn how to ride a bicycle, it seems that I ran many miles alongside each of them holding the bike straight and coaching them as they learned. I didn't always feel like running miles in the hot Louisiana summers but I did because I should have. I didn't always feel like being a parent but I did because I ought to have.

My need to pray insures my praise. Praise puts me into character of what God is used to. Revelation 4-5 gives us a glimpse of what heaven's praise is like. From the casting of crowns to the shouting of saints, He is never outside of the overwhelming praise of saints, angels, and the living ones. My approach to Him must seem fairly anemic without my giving Him the highest praise. I want to approach God in His worth, not in my dullness. When it is hardest to praise and pray, I must focus on praising and praying the hardest.

Praise brings a change of mood by redirecting my focus. Praise focuses on His greatness and takes my mind off of my pettiness.

Satan's world is negative, critical, gloomy and dark. Praise, focusing on the essence of who God is, puts evil into proper perspective and cuts the devil down to size.

There must be a level of confidence established in the heart in order to pray in powerful expectation. If Satan can bring doubt about our relationship with the Lord, he has been successful in spiritually grounding us. He only wants to confuse us enough for our confidence in prayer to be diminished.

There was once a farmer who battled with inconsistency in his walk with God because of doubt. One day he said to the Lord that he was settling his relationship with Him and at that point drove a large wooden stake down in one of his pastures. Once and for all, he gave himself wholly to the Lord. Ever after that, when the devil tempted the farmer with doubt, he simply glanced up at the stake and saw the marker post indicating his total abandonment to God's place in his life.

It may be important for the Christian, who is insecure in his walk with the Lord, to drive a stake down in prayer. Find God's will and agree with Him. Do the warfare. Fight through to the release that God has heard you. When doubt arises, show Satan the stake.

Mark 11:21 places the order of action when we pray with expectation. *"Therefore, I say to you, whatever things you ask when you pray, believe that you receive them, and you will have them."* We first believe then we receive. Receive in your heart first then, into your hand.

At this point, it is important to avoid faith tampering elements that will arise. Listening to negative, carnally minded people will tamper with faith. Receiving negative and evil reports about people from gossips will hinder faith. Reading circumstances as they seem to look will hinder faith. Consider the disciples after the crucifixion. All seemed lost and they lost faith. Discouragement is always ready to avail itself to the believer who is trending toward self-effort rather than the power of faith. At this point, some prefer to interfere rather than to intercede.

To pray with expectation, prayer must see from the correct vantage point. The instructions of Jesus to His developing disciples is found in Matthew 10:7-8, *"As you go, preach, saying, the kingdom of heaven is at hand. Heal the sick, cleanse the lepers, raise the dead, cast out demons."* The proper vantage point to see these things happen is the "kingdom of heaven." The needs were healing, cleansing, death, and the demonic. While there is no possible way for these men to have confidence that they could accomplish this from their own vantage point, the view from the kingdom of heaven changed all of the possibilities. No Biblical miracle ever happened without beginning with a desperate problem.

There are three elements involved in my praying. There is:

God – God conscious
Me – Self-conscious
Need – Problem conscious

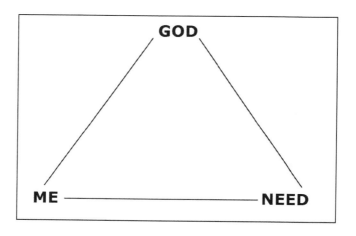

Whichever of these three vantage points that we pray from will determine the scope of the answer to our prayer.

To assure expected answers when I pray, I must first escape earthly bondages.

Self-conscious – how do I view self?
Problem conscious – Who bad is it?
God conscious – How able is God?

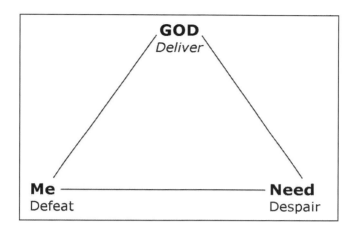

Will I pray from a point of defeat, despair, or deliverance?

To assure expected answers when I pray, I must first escape earthly bondages.

Our focus must be on the One who is our beginning and end. Hebrews 12:2 calls Jesus the author and finisher of our faith. We are to look to Him. When overwhelming needs arise, glance at your problem but gaze at your God.

The problem that I am facing that requires prayer is what God is pointing to. I am agreeing with Him and believing Him by faith. Faith will bring pleasure to God and will bring treasure to me. Hebrews 11:6.

Prevailing in Prayer
Chapter 7

It was so hot that it was difficult to pay attention. It was camp meeting time and into its third day. It was July in the deep South and the heat and humidity was high. I was fifteen years old. The camp entailed one preacher after another all day and into the night. The plain auditorium held twenty-five hundred people. There was no air conditioning and the benches were two by twelve boards clamped together. The windows were open but the sheer curtains hung perfectly still without a stirring of breeze. People were fanning with anything that could be improvised into a fan. The camp director came to the pulpit and said, "God wants one more preacher tonight but it is too hot in the building. Since God wants it, we will have it. I need some men to join me in the altar to ask God to cool the building." I sat up straight on my board bench. I had not heard this type of praying much.

Many men filled the altars and the director began to pray. "Lord, we want what you want. We want to hear more preaching but it is too hot. We need you to cool the building for us. We will wait a little bit to give you time."

I had never heard praying like this. The worship leader was asked to sing a couple of songs while we waited. It was during the second song that I heard the thunder in the distance. Then, the sheer curtains began to stir in a rare breeze. The hair stood up on the back of my neck. Within fifteen minutes, there came a heavy rain. The building cooled as though it was air conditioned. We could hardly hear the music for the sound of rain on the metal roof. When it had subsided, the director acted as though this was something seen every day. The next preacher stepped up and preached in a cool building. My perspective of prayer would never be the same.

James 5:16 says, *"The effective, fervent prayer of a righteous man avails much."* The next couple of verses detail some prayer events in the life of the prophet Elijah. When one goes back to the Old Testament account of these works, it should be noticed that everything that Elijah prayed were things that God told him was going to happen. He was praying what God had promised. The scriptures are replete with stories of answered prayers.

The confidence that gives the prayer warrior "hanging on" faith stems from the fact that God has made certain promises that our faith should stand on.

The promises of God are in place for our faith. The great worth of God's promises is that they establish God's will. God only answers within His will.

The power to prevail is stronger when we want the same thing that God wants. God's promises help us to know and anticipate an answer. If God has not promised it, don't expect it.

The promises of God that the praying saint embraces also exalt the name of Jesus. We know that there is no greater name to trust in. To pray in Jesus' name, with His promises in my heart, is a very powerful position with the Living God. The name of Jesus is a strong endorsement for my sanctified desire in prayer.

Standing on the promises of God in prayer releases the power of the Holy Spirit. Romans 8:26-27 teaches us that the Holy Spirit knows the heart of God and intercedes for us according to the will of God. The Spirit is a great advocate for us in our seeking the face of the Lord.

The Biblical pictures of those prevailing in prayer are awesome in their inspiration. Nearly every circumstance imaginable has been illustrated by the lives of real people.

Jacob is a picture of one who holds on. Genesis 32:22-32 tells this part of his story. He wrestled with the Lord all night and was changed. His injury from this fixed fight (it would have been easy for the Lord to end this quickly) was permanent. Hebrews 11:21 mentions that Jacob died leaning on a staff. He refused to let go until he was blessed. The testimony is that he had prevailed (verse 28). Some give up far too easily. Some are not willing to chance adversity or injury in order to prevail. How deep is your need and how important is the answer?

Rizpah is a picture of those who wait. Her story is in 2 Samuel 21:10-11. To prevail in prayer is to never give up praying. Luke 18:1 is the instruction of Jesus to pray and not faint. Rizpah's life took her from living in a palace to living on a rock beating the birds off of her dead sons. She waited until the King heard.

Moses showed us how to stand up. Exodus 32 gives us the picture of Moses standing up for the people in intercession and saving them from God's judgment. God told Moses that Moses' people had sinned (verse 7). Moses reminded God that they were actually God's people (verse 11) and Moses held God's hands from destroying them. This is praying with great boldness. This is how God expects us to approach Him (Hebrews 4:16).

While praying in prevailing power there are several principles to keep in mind. For example, our knowledge of prayer should not exceed our experience in prayer. If you know how to pray, then pray. Many know the principles of prayer but are they praying? We know God is able, but is He doing it? It is difficult for God to use one who knows more than he has experienced. We pray out of the overflow of God's word working in us.

In order to have confidence in prayer, our fellowship with God must be a priority. To begin a desperate prayer by saying, "Lord, I know it's been a long time since we talked..." will accomplish very little. Daniel 11:32 reminds us that the people who know their God shall be strong and do great exploits. It's too late to try to figure out how to load your gun in the middle of the war. Jesus said in John 10 that His sheep follow Him because they know His voice.

In order to prevail for an answer to prayer, our faith must exceed our impatience. We must be willing to stare the devil right in the face and keep calling out to God. When the answer is delayed (Daniel 9), we must not give up. If you know His promises, if you know His will, hold on, never give up, and keep on praying. Speak the promises out loud. Ask, seek, and knock but don't stop.

Prevailing in prayer is:

Hannah praying in the tabernacle.
Ruth begging Naomi.
Rachel crying, "Give me children or I die."
Hagar crying, "I can't watch my son die."
Daniel, whose only fault was that he prayed too much.
Joel crying, "Gather the people, call a fast, weep before God."
Jeremiah saying, "That my head were waters and my eyes a
    fountain of tears that I might weep day and night."
Elijah on Mount Carmel.
Elisha saying, "I will not leave you without the anointing."
Pentecost when they did nothing but pray for ten days.

Disciples saying, "Lord, teach us to pray." (not preach, sing, etc)
Paul with his back lacerated to the bone singing and praying.
Jesus with great drops of blood, clinging to God's will.

He has given us great and precious promises. 2 Peter 1:4

God's Presence In Prayer
Chapter 8

I reached my hand out from under the cover and found His strong hand. He gently held my hand as I listened to the struggling breath of my sick wife lying next to me. Sweet peace flooded my soul as I settled into the reality of His presence in the darkened room. His eyes locked on mine with such gentleness and security that my heart was at complete rest.

While in college, many years ago, I read a book written by a lay brother of the Carmelite Priory in Paris. His name was Brother Lawrence and he was a kitchen worker in the monastery. He lived from 1614 to 1691. His book remains in print entitled, <u>The Practice of the Presence of God</u>. He wrote in his chronicle about his imagining the reality of the presence of Jesus with him in the kitchen as he worked. The fellowship that he had with Jesus was very real and the Lord's presence was strong.

I later read a message by the Scottish preacher Alexander Whyte (1836-1921) in which he spoke of sitting at his table with Jesus seated just across from him while he spoke to the Lord.

I began to think again of the promises the Lord made about always being with us and never leaving us. This is the reality of life with Him.

Since those early days, I have always used a sanctified imagination to have Jesus seated on my bed at night, in the seat next to me in my truck, walking with me, and various other scenarios. I seldom ever begin a prayer until I see Him in my mind and can speak directly to Him.

Some will have trouble with this and believe it to be mystical but for me it changed how I pray. Prayer is personal, His presence, though unseen, is so very real to me.

David wrote in Psalm 19:14, *"Let the words of my mouth and the meditation of my heart be acceptable in Your sight, O Lord, my strength and my redeemer."* The meditation of my heart (imagination) is the birth place of my words. Jesus taught that it is what comes out of us that is important. The mouth speaks out of the abundance of the heart. Since God has blessed me with an active imagination, I have purposed to use this imagination to realize His actual presence and practice that presence regularly, especially in prayer.

As fallen beings, our thoughts must be purified in order to be acceptable to the Lord. The Bible normally presents the imagination of people as a dark part of their existence. It is noted in Psalm 36:4, *"He plots trouble while on his bed."* In the fourteen times that imagination is mentioned in the Scriptures, thirteen times it is portrayed as evil. Our imagination actually allows us to sin privately without exposure. God doesn't separate thoughts and deeds in the darkness of men's lives. If the imagination is constantly on evil things, Satan will eventually set up the circumstance for our thoughts to become reality. This is the progressive nature of sin.

The sanctification of the Christian involves his whole being. To be sanctified is to be set aside for a special purpose. When the Holy Spirit sanctifies the believer, the imagination becomes sanctified also. 1 Thessalonians 5:23 says, *"May the God of peace Himself sanctify you completely; and may your whole spirit, soul, and body be preserved blameless at the coming of our Lord Jesus Christ."* Those who live the faith with only their body tend to be legalists. Those who live the faith with only the spirit tend to be liberals.

The balanced believer lives a life of faith in combination of both body and spirit through the soul. The soul includes the mind, will, and emotions. It is a sanctified imagination (mind) that I use in prayer to experience the reality of His presence.

Pure thinking through a sanctified imagination yields creative service. Creativity is born in the imagination. Someone dreams a building design like the Empire State Building then, someone builds what was dreamed. The Statue of Liberty was once a spark of creativity in someone's imagination that later became a reality. God did this very thing in forming the universe. He thought it, then, spoke the dream into reality. Our imagination gives us possibilities beyond what is and envisions what could be.

This type of creativity in the imagination keeps the Christian's service fresh. It is said that eighty percent of churches in America are plateaued or in decline. Much of this can be attributed to lack of envisioning what could be over what is. Some see things as they are and ask "why?" Others see things that could be and asks "why not?" Simon Peter preached on the Day of Pentecost that, in the ending age, young men would have visions and old men would dream dreams (Acts 2:17). Spiritual imagination, purified dreaming, and envisioning comes from the Holy Spirit. What could be done in your home, job, or church if there were more imaginative dreamers?

It is my experience that meditation brings the Bible's spiritual truth into reality. This brings life to God's word. In 1977, Suzie and I traveled to the land of Israel. It would be the first of many trips for us. While I walked in the land of the Bible, Biblical truth began to come alive in my mind. I stood in the dry brook that had separated the armies of the Israelites under Saul from the armies of the Philistines under Goliath. As I stood in the brook bed with a smooth stone in my hand, the battle became real in my mind. I could envision the scene before my eyes. I heard Goliath's roar of intimidation. I saw the trembling Israelites. I watched a young shepherd boy emerge from the army of Saul and walk toward the brook. He bent down and carefully selected several stones. He placed them in a leather pouch. One stone was placed in the sling that he held in his hand. He climbed the shallow bank of the brook toward the Philistine army. Words were exchanged and I heard the whoosh of leather strings as the sling rapidly circled his head. There was a snap, followed by a dull thud, as the stone sank into the giant's forehead. There came a crashing sound as the giant, in his heavy armor, fell face down at the feet of the boy. A roar of jubilation arose from the Israeli army as the dynamics of the standoff had completely changed. This really happened in David's day. It happened again in my mind.

As I read my Bible, I have seen the tears of Father Abraham trickling down his gray beard as he lifted the knife of sacrifice over his only son, Isaac. I have heard blind Bartimaeus crying out in the street to Jesus for healing. I have felt the heat of the day, tasted the dust of the street in the air, felt the press of the crowd, and stood in the thick silence as Jesus gave sight to the beggar. I saw the tears and heard the shouts at the healing. I have stood and looked up at the cross upon which my Savior hung and heard the weeping of many as the skies darkened. I try to walk into my Bible every time I read its stories. I take such joy in using my sanctified imagination to experience the truth of God's word.

In experiencing the Bible this way, the academic aspect of His word is removed and it becomes a living word. The vagueness is lifted and excitement fills my heart. When I read my Bible, I revel in its reality.

This type of imagining helps prayer to become genuine communication with the God I love with all of my heart. Through this type of praying, I am able to experience the reality of the Lord's presence. I practice His presence in my bed, in my truck, at my table, on my job, in my praying, and in my worship.

Sanctified imagination strips away empty tradition from my prayer life. It allows me to put my heart into conversation with God. I am able to experience the peace and love of His countenance. It removes idle words and vain phrases from my prayers. I no longer pray with empty rote and tradition. I can worship in heaven, rest at His feet, hold His hand in the night, or lay my head in His lap.

My mother was a very strong disciplinarian. She was quick to act when there was unacceptable behavior from us children. She was old school in her rearing of children.

I don't remember the infraction but one evening she sent me to bed with no supper because of something that I said or did. I have no doubt that I was in the wrong but the reaction was swift and strong.

I lay in my bed that evening hungry and rejected. I was crying softly, probably in self-pity. My older sister Sandy slipped into my dark room later that night when she heard my whimpering. Sandy and I have been close friends all of our lives. She sat on the side of my bed and cradled my head in her lap. She wiped my eyes with the bed sheet and pushed the hair off of my forehead. She said to me, "Someday, Steve, I will have a house of my own. You can come live with me and never cry again." I took such comfort in that.

Through the years, following that long night, I have rested my sorrowing head in the lap of my Savior and have heard Him say so many times, "Someday, Steve, you can come live with me and never cry again."

It has been a very long time since I have prayed, communicated, or simply visited with the Lord without seeing Him right by my side. He smiles often and I love His presence.

Praying For The Sick
Chapter 9

Genevieve was forty-nine years old. She was in our church and was a bold, demonstrative worshiper who loved preaching. She was divorced and lived alone. She approached me one Wednesday evening with a doctor's report stating that she had serious bone cancer. Another woman in our church, who worked in this doctor's office, confirmed the cancer report.

I asked Genevieve how she wanted me to pray for her. She said that she wanted to live to celebrate her fiftieth birthday. With other pastors on our staff, I anointed her with oil and prayed over her. As of this writing she is still alive. This happened over twenty years ago. When she returned to her oncologist, it was the usual story after God heals. He had no idea how the cancer left but she was cancer free without any treatment. Our friend, who worked in the doctor's office, confirmed the cancer free diagnosis. She had seen the before and after scans side by side.

Beryl had been a Christian since childhood. He was now a Bible teacher, deacon, and Christian businessman. He was very sick. As with many in the past, he asked for healing prayer according to James 5. Several men joined with me and prayed over him, anointing him with oil. It took only a few months for the sickness to take his life.

Why is there healing for some and not for others? It is a question that I have pondered for many years. I don't know if I will ever figure it out. There are some things about God that I will never understand. God is far too big for my limited mind. I have combed the scriptures to find as many principles that I can about the Lord's healing of the sick.

When one looks at Biblical illnesses, they seem to fall into three categories. There are diseases of sensory impairment. These include blindness, deafness, dumbness, mania, and speech impairment. Another grouping of Biblical diseases includes mobility impairment. This includes lameness, paralysis, withered limbs, and deformity. A third grouping is that of skin diseases including leprosy, hemorrhaging, and worm infestation.

There are three causes of Biblical diseases that are plain in scripture. Of course, it begins with sin. We live in a fallen, sick world. Everything is on a course of death. Much of the disease that is present in the world stems from the entry of sin into a perfect world. When Jesus healed the man at the pool of Bethesda, He told him to *"Stop sinning or something worse may happen to you."* (John 5:14). The Holy Spirit said that many were weak, sick, or dead because they did not properly discern the Lord's body in the Lord's Supper (1 Corinthians 11:30).

God also causes disease in certain cases. Think of the plagues of Egypt. There is also the death of Ananias and his wife Sapphira (Acts 5) that was the result of lying to the Holy Spirit. Consider what God did to Herod in Acts 12. The story of Elymas the sorcerer is recorded in Acts 13. It should be noted in these accounts that specific sins are noted and did not happen simply because of the general nature of sin.

The third cause of Biblical diseases stems from the demonic. Satan's strategy is to kill, steal, and destroy. Sickness certainly is included in this strategy. The Bible speaks of demonic bondage (See my book on spiritual warfare – Confronting the Enemy). Luke 13 gives us the account of the woman who was held in the bondage of infirmity for eighteen years. Mark 9 reveals a lad with a mute spirit. In fact, twenty-five percent of the diseases listed in the Gospel of Mark are related to demonic causes.

It should be observed at this point that most diseases spoken of in the Bible could be classified as natural. Caution should be shown when thinking of sickness. Not all of them are God's judgment or Satan's work. This entire world is dying. Every animal, tree, bacteria, and human is dying. Romans 8:22 indicates that the entire created world groans under the weight of sin.

When the New Testament is searched in order to find a cure for sickness, it should be pointed out that, while many of the sick were healed, not all of them were. Trophimus at Miletus was not healed (2 Timothy 4:20). Epiphroditus was sick but recovered naturally (Philippians 2:25). Paul could not heal Timothy's stomach problem (1 Timothy 5:23).

This is a good place to learn the difference between sickness and suffering in the Bible. There is a distinction made between suffering and sickness in James 5:14-15.

New Testament suffering usually stemmed from outside sources, mostly from evil people. Jesus suffered but was not sick. Paul had a thorn that brought suffering (2 Corinthians 12) and persecution (verse 10) was from others. There was the woman who had suffered at the hands of doctors (Mark 5:26).

The purpose of suffering is two-fold: Education (Hebrews 5:7) and testing (Hebrews 2:18).

Four possible responses should be made by Christians in suffering. Philippians 1:29 indicates that it is a privilege to enter into suffering for Jesus' sake. We have actually been given permission to suffer for Him.

Philippians 3:10 encourages that suffering is a doorway to blessings. James 5:7-11 teaches that suffering develops patient endurance. Finally, and perhaps the most difficult response, 1 Peter 4:13 provides that the Christian should rejoice in suffering.

When the circumstance is sickness rather than suffering, what should the believer do? James 5:14-18 details the protocol to be used by believers in seeking healing. It is important for the sick one to be rightly aligned and under the covering of a local church. This provides a collection of those who can and will believe God. It provides discernment and agreement about the prayer for healing. The procedure in asking is that the sick one should approach the elders, asking for prayer. Usually the term elders is meant to represent pastors or spiritually mature ones in the body of the church.

When the elders pray over the sick one, the ailing one is to be anointed with oil according to verse 15. The word "save" means to deliver, heal, or cure. The picture of anointing oil in the scripture most often indicates the Holy Spirit. It should be understood that the oil is merely symbolic. It is not special oil with healing properties in it like medicine. Usually leaders use olive oil but I have known other types of oil used, even oil off of a dipstick, depending upon the availability of oil. Olive oil with herbs or spices, blessed by spiritual leaders, or other qualities, has no special power above regular oil. Oil is a picture, a type of the Holy Spirit only. Its purpose is to inspire faith by its representation.

This is also a time for the sick one to discern any sin in his life that may be a cause of sickness or may hinder the Holy Spirit from working in his healing. Repentance, confession, and renunciation will remove the sin but perhaps not the consequences of it.

Consideration given to healing in the New Testament must hold in perspective that God may choose to heal in miracle or medicinal mode, if He decides to heal at all. In Acts28:8-9 is found an interesting principle that is not easily discerned by reading the Bible in the English language. It is the account of the Apostle Paul and the medical doctor, Luke, dealing with sickness on the island of Malta. Publius was a leading citizen of the island and he was sick with fever and dysentery. Paul laid his hands on him and prayed. The context indicates that his healing was immediate. It is safe to assume this was a healing miracle. The Greek word "iaomai" is used in this passage. The next verse states that after that, the rest of the sick on the island came and were also healed. The Greek word used for healed here is "therapeuo". The English word therapy comes from this word. Dr. Luke, with his medicine, was healing the sick alongside Paul who was healing by miracle. What does it matter how God heals, by miracle or medicine? Jesus is the Healer. Healed is healed no matter the process.

Why does God heal some and not others? Only God, in His sovereignty knows. I pray the James 5 protocol over the sick unless God tells me to pray differently. It is always the beginning point with me. What happens from there is God's decision.

Fasting – The Spiritual Side
Chapter 10

Suzie and I began to sense that God was going to send us to a new area to minister for Him. We had served in the area before and had never thought about going back. We were serving five hundred miles from that point now in a wonderful church. As a deep pressure in our hearts continued to build about this change, we decided that we would fast and seek the Lord diligently about it. We didn't want to miss Him in this. Suzie and I had been fasting for five days when the release came. We were certain that God was going to send us to the designated area. We broke the fast and waited for the details. Shortly after this, a church from this area talked with us about coming to help them. We were very familiar with this church and loved many of the people in it. Much to our surprise, it did not work out. When that was settled, Suzie said to me, "We got a word from God so this doesn't mean that we aren't going to this area, it means that we are not going to that church." She was exactly right. In a few days, I received a phone call from someone that I did not know. He asked us to come to the area of interest and plant a new church. This was our answer. We gave birth to a new church and stayed a number of years with the blessings of Jesus.

Fasting has played a great part in our lives. We have fasted for one day each week in the past, simply to have a focused prayer day. We have fasted for special events, people to be touched by the Holy Spirit, and have fasted in order to do spiritual warfare. Although we grew up in church, neither of us had ever fasted before the Lord. Our searching the Bible turned out to be a great lesson that changed our lives.

The first question that is usually asked about this subject is "Why should I fast?" Surprisingly, the answer to this question is plainly evident in the Bible.

The easiest answer is that I should fast because Jesus expects me to. The teaching that Jesus did about fasting is found in the opening chapters of the New Testament. In Matthew 4 there is the wilderness temptation where we find Jesus fasting for forty days then being tempted by Satan. Two chapters later, Matthew 6, Jesus teaches about giving, praying, and fasting. In verse two Jesus said, "**When** you give…" In verse 5 He says, "**When** you pray…" In verse 16, Jesus says, "**When** you fast…" Note that in each case He said when, not if. Fasting is not anymore optional than prayer or giving. It is expected of Christians to have times of fasting.

I should also make fasting part of my life simply because the times will require it. Matthew 9:15 asks us,

"Can the wedding guests mourn as long as the bridegroom is with them? The days will come when the bridegroom is taken away from them, and then they will fast." We are living in the age now when Jesus said that fasting would be a part of our lives.

I should fast in order to focus on ministering to the Lord. We read in Acts 13:2, *"While they were ministering to the Lord and fasting, the Holy Spirit said, 'Set apart for Me Barnabas and Saul for the work to which I have called them."* While ministering to the Lord with fasting, clear direction was given.

There are three types of fasting that the Holy Spirit lists in the Bible. Daniel practiced a *partial* fast. A partial fast is a restricted diet. It is agreeing to restrict certain foods from the diet. In Daniel 1:8, Daniel restricted certain foods from the kings table. This fast was built upon purpose and was successful in its purpose.

The second type of fast mentioned the *normal* fast. This type of fast is the most common fast mentioned in the Bible. It is the type of fast that Jesus followed in Matthew 4:2. It is a fast of drinking only water for a given period of time. I have known some who have fasted like this for forty days just as Jesus did. It can be described as a fast of no food, only water.

Then there is the *absolute* fast that Paul practiced in Acts 9:9. It is a fast of no food or water. Evidently, this fast cannot be for a very long time simply because of the body's need for water. God will never lead one to harm his body.

With these fasts typified by Bible characters, there were both public and private times of fasting practiced. A public fast took place when a people or group were called together and publicly challenged to fast for a certain purpose. A call to this type fast is illustrated in Joel 2:15. There is also a regular fast. This fast is found recorded in Jeremiah 36:6. It is a fast that occurs on a regular basis. Many years ago, I fasted this way with a staff pastor every Monday. We prayed together, went soul winning, or did other ministries in the name of the Lord. It is a recurring fast that happens on a regular basis.

There are varying reasons for entering into a fast that God has called one to. To look into the lives of those Biblical characters who fasted, it causes us to realize that fasting kicks our prayer life up a notch in intensity and provides greater focus.

In the Bible, we learn that fasting is done for the purpose of personal consecration. This is the fast the Jesus followed in the wilderness before His temptation. Before He launched His public ministry, He spent forty days before God in fasting and prayer getting ready for what was planned from the foundation of the world. The early church did this before sending Barnabas and Saul away on their mission to other cities and nations (Acts 13:3). David fasted for this purpose often as seen in Psalm 69:10. Fasting brings with it a certain humility that is imperative for serving the Lord.

Fasting also helps in our being heard by God. Ezra 8:23 says, *"So we fasted and pleaded with our God about this and He granted our request."* Isaiah 58 is the fasting chapter of the Old Testament with many promises to the one who answers God's call to fast. In verses 4 and 9, we find these words, *"You will not fast as you do this day, to make your voice heard on high. Then shall you call, and the LORD will answer; You shall cry, and He will say, 'Here I am'".* When just regular praying doesn't seem to be getting any traction, fasting seems to loosen things up in order for God to answer. Desperate praying moves one into fasting.

Interestingly, according to the scriptures, fasting sometimes changes God's mind in conditional judgment. We have Jonah's story to illustrate this truth. God told Jonah to preach to the Ninevites a message that warned of destruction unless they repented. A deadline was established for repentance. Jonah preached and the people repented of their sin. Jonah 3:5 details that they fasted in their repentance and Jonah 3:10 tells of God's changed mind. This can hold true for conditional judgment but not for all circumstances. Moses interceded to God on behalf of the people in their rebellion (Exodus 32) and God changed His mind about destroying them. David sought God with fasting about his sick child (2 Samuel 12) but

God allowed the child to die in spite of David's praying with fasting.

Fasting is helpful in freeing the spiritually bound. Isaiah 58:6 says, *"Is this not the fast that I have chosen: To loose the bonds of wickedness, to undo the heavy burdens, to let the oppressed go free, and that you break every yoke?"* We have seen multiple bondages broken, even in our own families. We have seen the lost claimed and saved through fasting. We have seen warfare successfully release prisoners to freedom. This is a powerful weapon in standing against the kingdom of darkness.

Fasting is sometimes useful in receiving revelation from God. This is the reason that Daniel prayed with fasting (Daniel 9:3, 21-22). After fasting, Paul had a word from God that the ship he was on would go down but no life would be lost (Acts

27:21-24). An angel stood by him and assured him of God's truth.

One other purpose for fasting is to subdue the flesh. I have found that when I am fasting, the flesh will whine and complain but in time, it will come into submission to my spirit and its power to control areas of my life is greatly diminished. learned this on the first seven day fast that I entered into. I was amazed at how docile my flesh had become by the end of the fast. It gives power to my spirit to dominate the lusts, drives, and demands of my flesh.

Fasting is not synonymous with starving. It has spiritual purpose and brings us to a level of power and victory that just regular praying will not attain. It opens up a whole new world to those who will master it.

Fasting – The Physical Side
Chapter 11

I walked into the student union one day while in college. My high school friend, David, was sitting at a piano playing beautiful music. I sat beside him on the bench and began to play alongside him. After playing together for several minutes, I offered to buy him lunch.

David smiled and said, "Not today, Steve, I'm fasting."

I said, "Fasting?, Tell me about that."

He said, "I don't know much about it, I just fast at times when I really want to seek the Lord."

I said, "Then I will fast with you."

My heart was pure but I failed miserably.

That short conversation launched a desire in me to know about fasting. This desire took me through years of seeking and experiencing.

What I quickly learned was that if I did not prepare myself physically to fast, I probably would not be very successful in my fast.

The Psalmist David said, *"My knees are weak through fasting; my body has become gaunt, with no fat."* (Psalm 109:24) The physical aspect of fasting must be considered alongside the spiritual aspect.

How should one prepare physically for a fast? I must prepare both my body and my mind. For me, a fast begins with a continuing impression that God is calling me to a fast. Isaiah 58:5 indicates that a time of fasting is chosen by God. Fasting is not for ourselves (Isaiah 58:3). When I sense that God is calling me into a time of fasting, I begin to prepare my mind to rearrange my life to accommodate what He is calling me to.

I once began to feel the impression that God was calling me to isolate myself to Him with a seven day fast. I explained to Him that I could not fast the week He had chosen. I had committed myself to a luncheon meeting with the board of a mission organization upon which I sat. I had a lunch meeting with the worship leader of our entire denomination. I had staff meetings in which food was always a part and other social engagements with food built into it. The Holy Spirit brought deep conviction to me about putting Him off for food. I canceled every meeting except the meeting with the worship leader. He was flying in from another state to meet with me about some matters. My meeting with him was on the sixth day of my fast. I went to lunch with him and his companion and sat visiting with them as they slopped white gravy over huge chicken fried steaks with bread, veggies, and sweet tea. I had passed the hunger stage and had no problem sitting with them. My mind had settled into the fasting mode.

Preparing my mind means that I must put the importance of food in its proper place. Many live to eat rather than eating to live. Eating is one of the most addictive habits that we develop in life. There is a mental bondage to food since we have been eating at least three times a day for as long as we have been alive. Most drug addicts don't use that often. I must control food and not let food control me.

I learned early on that God has certain attitudes about food lusts and food addictions. Exodus 16:3 indicates that a lust for food can lead to resentment of God's actions and deliverance. The lust for food may also cause rebellion against God and

His leaders according to Numbers 11:4, 5. In Numbers 21:5, we find people rebelling against the provision of God because of food lusts. It is even possible for the judgment of God to come upon those who use food as the measurement of the depth of their obedience as seen in Psalm 78:18-31. My mind must come into submission to the Holy Spirit.

Once the mind is brought into submission, the body must be prepared. There are some steps to take that help cope with the discomfort of doing without food. Headaches are common in the beginning of a fast. Usually this is from caffeine and refined sugar withdrawal. This makes the fasting experience very uncomfortable. To avoid this, caffeine and refined sugar should be removed from the diet at least two days before fasting, longer if possible. This withdrawal can happen within the first hours of a fast so even if one is fasting for only 24 hours, a headache could be a problem.

Another helpful act would be to avoid dense or heavy protein for a couple of days before beginning a fast. Beef or pork takes time to digest and hang around the digestive tract for days. Remember, at any one time, most of us have three to six meals inside of us. Some with slow metabolisms may have up to ten meals inside. Protein is important to our function but one would be better served by eating legumes, protein drinks, or other sources of lighter forms of protein. Soft vegetables and fruit, eaten for a couple of days before fasting, will help to grind the residue of meals on through.

If fasting is a new concept for you and you cannot conceive of eating no food for a time, it may be best to build up to it. For example, miss one meal a day for several days in order to break the mental habit of eating.

This also helps in getting used to the empty feeling that accompanies fasting. After several days of missing one meal a day, miss two meals in a day for several days. This way one is easing into a new mindset that the body and mind must adjust to. If you fail, don't be discouraged. Most that begin fasting have trouble at first.

Once my mind and body are prepared, it is time to identify my motives. Fasting for the purpose of seeing how long one can go will not be successful. I always set down my purpose in fasting before I begin. I go so far as writing it down. If I do not have a purpose when fasting, I will not be able to know if the fast was successful. A time of fasting should always have a purpose, a focus. It must be a fast that God has chosen.

We were once reassigned to a new ministry area in another state. We had lived for years in the same place. We had a house to sell in the former area and also had to find a place to live in the new area. The new church that we had been called to had graciously agreed to pay our house note for a certain number of months until our former house in another state sold so that we would not be responsible for two house notes. The former house was in a terribly depressed economy and as the months rolled by, there was little to no interest in it by prospective buyers. As our deadline was approaching, there arose a deep concern that we would be required to pay two notes, a situation that would put great stress on our home. While we had been asking God to bring a buyer for our house, there seemed to be no prospect of it selling soon. I decided that I would fast before the Lord in order to better focus on our need in prayer. I began a fast, praying that God would bring someone to buy our house. There was nothing happening for six days. On the seventh day of my fast, we signed a contract and sold our former home. We closed on the sale only days before the deadline. A seven day fast, praying before the Lord had brought about the unlikely. My motive was to keep the pressure from our home while establishing a new ministry.

I have found that when the Holy Spirit calls me to a fast, His timing is impeccable. Because He knows all things, He establishes the time according to His will. I once felt called to a six day fast for a time of seeking the Lord about a prospective ministry opportunity. Because of pressing matters, I postponed what I knew should have been the beginning day of the fast. I waited four days to begin. On the third day of the fast, I came down with a stomach virus and was very sick for several days. I missed the six days of fasting and had only succeeded in fasting for two days. Had I begun on schedule, I would have been finished with the fast before I became sick. God knew I would be sick and called me to fast before the sickness arrived. I lost the fast and made it up later after I was well again. When the Lord calls, He knows what He is doing.

What should be done while the fast is in progress? There are some considerations to be made while fasting. There are certain physical principles to consider in a fast. For example, if one is on medicine that must be taken, it is possible that a partial fast is in order. It would be wise to clear the possibility of a fast with your doctor. I have had a physical condition since childhood called hypoglycemia. It is a situation where my blood sugar can drop in just a few minutes and cause severe discomfort, mood swings, and cognitive impairment. When that happens, I must eat protein immediately or it is possible to have some critical health problems. This blood drop usually happens by missing a meal or eating refined sugar then going too long without protein to stabilize my blood sugar. I have had some rough times dealing with this condition. The curious side of this is that when I have been called to a multi-day fast, I have never had a single problem with this. It is simply the protection of the Healer while obeying His call to a fast.

There are certain mental facts that I must cling to. Some do not understand fasting and equate it with starving. They are afraid that if several meals are missed that there will be powerful health problems arise. Truthfully, a healthy human can go several weeks without food without damaging their health. Water is another matter. Only a few days without water can cause some detrimental health conditions. Fasting is not the same as starving. When fasting, the body is cleansing itself. When fasting, the body is able to burn away wastes, fats, and decaying tissue. Starvation sets in when healthy cells are being consumed by the body, when the body begins to eat itself. Going without food is not starvation until the body begins to consume its own healthy tissue.

There are several actions that will enhance the spiritual experience in fasting. Some are simply practical in nature.
It is helpful to avoid watching TV when fasting. A great percentage of commercials on TV appeals to the appetite. It is smart to avoid being around food for the first few days. I find it helpful to avoid the presence or smells of food for the first three or four days of an extended fast. I count the growling of an empty stomach as a call to pray and pray every time my stomach rumbles. I try to carry on a regular schedule while fasting to avoid drawing attention to myself in fasting. Idle time tends to be a fasting killer. If left alone, the mind

will dwell on all the food it is missing. Any capitulation to the flesh will weaken resolve. This is why Paul said it is good to abstain from marital sex while fasting (1 Corinthians 7:5). There must always be a purpose in fasting.

Someone who is experienced in fasting knows what to expect. Had I known earlier what to expect from my body when I first began to fast, I would not have become discouraged. If one fasts for more than two days, physical changes will take place. Even if a fast is only for hours, it is helpful to know what to expect. The most logical aspect to be aware of is hunger. Even if only one meal is missed, there will be emptiness and hunger. This is a new sensation for many because most eat often enough to keep from experiencing either.

When one fasts for three or more days, the hunger increases exponentially because the body is in the process of switching fuel systems from external to internal. Blood sugar must adjust to the new, low grade fuel. There may be sensitivity to cold. There certainly will be a great temptation, even desperation to eat and break the fast. Friends or family who are not savvy about fasting will try to convince the faster to eat and stop starving themselves. Their concern is real but not grounded in truth. The longer the fast continues there may be dizziness upon standing up quickly. Headaches may be a problem until the caffeine and sugar withdrawals are over. Be careful about taking headache meds on an empty stomach. After several days, the tongue may turn white and cottony. When ketosis begins to happen, the breath may become unpleasant. It may help to lightly brush the tongue and rinse with water. Be careful of breath mints or toothpaste. Brush with baking soda and salt instead. Most toothpastes and mints contain sugar and even in small amounts these could break the fast or hinder ketosis. Truthfully, the novice faster can expect to be generally miserable since the flesh has always had its way with food up until now. While fasting, time will move as slow as molasses at Christmas so it is profitable to continue on with normal activities to keep busy.

When is the fast to be broken? If a predetermined length of time was not set beforehand, one must be sensitive to receive a release from God to end the fast. Sometimes the Holy Spirit has given me a specific time to fast. I know that there are some Christians who do not believe that God speaks to them like this and I have compassion for them since they are living well beneath their privilege. Sometimes the answer to prayer will bring about the end to a fast as in Daniel 10. There are times when God will give His peace that He has heard and will act even though the answer will not be immediate. When that release comes, it is permissible to break the fast. I once fasted to pray for a situation in my son's life. After four days, I received a release from the Spirit that God had heard and would answer. I broke the fast although it was several days before the answer manifested itself. This allows the fast to be broken without guilt or a feeling of failure.

In the breaking of the fast one should use common sense. When I was a teenager, preaching in small churches on the Louisiana coast, my pastor called our church to a weekend fast to pray for an upcoming revival effort. I had begun to learn about fasting at that point but had never experienced a three day fast. I felt lead to participate. I began the fast on Friday. I was scheduled to preach on Sunday at FBC Grand Chenier, Louisiana. This church was on the coastal shelf of the Gulf of Mexico. After services, my friend Neil Crane, invited me to his house for lunch. He grilled some of the thickest, juiciest steaks that I had ever tasted in my life. I ate like a starving person. I paid a price for that. My stomach had not had anything but pure water for two and a half days. My digestive tract went into full rebellion and stress. I learned from that experience to use wisdom in breaking a multi-day fast. When has a hungry teenaged boy ever been wise with food?

I am not a dietician or a physician. I only speak out of the overflow of experience. If a fast is only for a meal or two, even twenty-four to thirty-six hours, it is permissible to resume normal eating habits (in moderation) immediately to break the fast. Eat moderately and wisely without giving in to the temptation of "catching up" and stuffing yourself. Pay attention to any signs of discomfort.

If three days or more is involved in fasting with only water intake, more care should be taken. Avoid meat for the first day and eat vegetables cooked softly or raw. The more fasting becomes a part of life, the easier it is for the body to ease back into a normal dietary routine.

If the fast is over ten days long, ease back into a normal diet within a week, watching for signs of overdoing it. Drink juices or vegetable shakes for the first day then soft cooked vegetables, legumes, and meat ground or chewed well after that. My wife Suzie once fasted with only water for twenty-six days. She took about a week to get back to a normal diet.

Suzie and I once were called into a fast together for a friend who was lost. We had been welcomed into her life. On the fifth day of our fast, the Holy Spirit affirmed to us that she would be saved. We were released from the fast. On a whim, we drove to a little greasy hamburger joint that we liked and each of us had a cheeseburger. That probably cut across wise thinking but fasting was such a part of our lives that we sailed through with no discomfort or consequences. The cheeseburgers were wonderful.

I had to learn to keep a few principles in mind when I first began to fast. I had to get used to the feeling of emptiness. Most are not used to this feeling and mistake it for hunger. Water helps with this. Regular drinking of water helps to wash out the debris being discarded by the system through fasting.

I realized early on that much of our eating is social. I had to get used to breaking this trend. Eating is also habitual. We eat because it is noon, not because we are hungry. I must forgo eating for the clock.

I also learned that my body, my flesh, is like a spoiled child. It is demanding in its desire for satisfaction. My mind will attempt to manipulate me into cheating on a fast. I remember learning this once when I was on a multi-day fast. Several days into the fast, while driving, I passed a fast food restaurant. My mind began its manipulation.

I thought, "I may have a wreck and die. That means I may never get to eat fried chicken again".

That seems ridiculous now but, at the time, it was graveyard serious. It is important to stay away from food and to avoid thinking or dreaming about food.

One should not be surprised if attacks from Satan come during these times of focused prayer and waiting on the Lord. My first serious attack from the demonic came to me during a time of fasting as a young man. It was in the middle of the night and I was not expecting it. I was taken completely by surprise. I am wise to his ways now and not surprised nor intimidated.

Beware of spiritual arrogance when fasting. Jesus said that the Pharisees loved to be seen in their fasting and loud praying. Suzie and I have made it a practice not to share that we are fasting with anyone except each other or those who have committed themselves to fast with us, following the sentiment of 1 Corinthians 7:5.

The most important aspect of fasting is to believe God, listen to God, and to subdue the flesh.

Some of God's greatest prayer warriors included fasting in their arsenal of weapons. God hears those who seek Him with all that they are.